IMAGES
of America

HISPANICS IN CONCHO

ON THE COVER: Taken around 1950, this photograph shows the widest swath of community members gathered together in Concho, Arizona. From left to right are (first row) Carlos "Charlie" or "Sonny" (Gonzales) Durán, Don Barreras, Lancaster "Lanky" Candelaria Jr., unidentified, Lucy Candelaria, unidentified, Emma (Durán) Padilla, and Porfirio "Porfie" Padilla; (second row) unidentified, Pedro Román Candelaria, Preciliano Candelaria, and Johnny "Kiddy" Padilla. (Courtesy of Román Candelaria.)

IMAGES
of America

HISPANICS IN CONCHO

Vanessa Fonseca-Chávez and Angela Perea-Murphy

ARCADIA
PUBLISHING

ISBN 978-1-4671-6267-8

Published by Arcadia Publishing
Charleston, South Carolina

Printed in the United States of America

Library of Congress Control Number: 2025938697

For all general information, please contact Arcadia Publishing:
Telephone 843-853-2070
Fax 843-853-0044
E-mail sales@arcadiapublishing.com

Visit us on the Internet at www.arcadiapublishing.com

*This book is dedicated to the people of Concho
and to their families, past and present.*

Contents

Acknowledgments

Concho has a magic of its own, safely tucked in the surrounding hills. We wrote this book because we believed in the importance of preserving the stories of Concho. We are both grateful to the community for taking us in, in different ways, and for allowing us to learn from you and share your photographs with a wider audience. Thanks to Arcadia Publishing and Caitrin Cunningham, our editor, for guiding us through this process. Thank you to the University of Texas at Austin Center for Mexican American Studies/Voces Oral History Collaborative Fellowship, which provided the opportunity to capture video oral history interviews and scanned photographs and documents in the summer of 2023. Most of the photographs in this book are a result of this collaboration. Thank you to Maggie Rivas-Rodríguez and her team for believing in Concho and learning alongside us.

I would like to thank Vanessa, my coauthor. Without her, my dream of becoming an author would have never become reality. I thank God for putting me in the right place and at the right time—in Concho. I thank all the Catholic priests who inspired me and those who did not. From them was knitted the strong fabric of my own faith. I thank Pat, my husband, for believing in me and thinking I am capable of anything. I love you. Rae, Brue, Tim, Gwyn, Ginny, and Kevin, my children, encouraged me to write a book and not look back. Grandchildren and great-grandchildren, this book is for you. I hope you learn to love history as much as I do.

—Angela Perea-Murphy

To everyone in Concho who has offered me, my students, and my collaborators a meal, a good conversation, a seat in a pew, or a place to rest, thank you. I am so grateful. Thank you to Max and Hope, who first introduced me to community members and who have become good friends/*familia*. Thank you to Angela, my coauthor, who responded enthusiastically to my request to write this book together. Lastly, thank you to my family and to my husband, who are always supportive of my scholarly meandering.

—Vanessa Fonseca-Chávez

INTRODUCTION

Concho the Enchanted Pearl: A History of Concho, Arizona (1981) is the most utilized community resource for understanding the early origins of Concho. E.M. DeGlane, who compiled the book, served as a historian for the now-defunct Concho Historical Society and was a regular contributor to a newspaper column titled "Concho Chatter" for more than 30 years. In his column he wrote about agriculture, the New Mexican Hispano families who founded Concho, and the daily happenings of the community that he cared about deeply, as do many of those who descend from the initial families who migrated to the area in the later part of the 19th century. According to Jo Baeza (2005), "Concho is the oldest continuously lived-in community in the White Mountains not on a reservation."

A version of how Concho came to be is often shared amongst Concho's rooted community. While this is documented in greater detail in DeGlane's book, the narrative generally is as follows: In the first part of the 19th century, a raiding party of Apaches in present-day northeastern Arizona captured some boys from Cubero, in present-day northwestern New Mexico. One of them was brought back to the White Mountains and given to a widowed woman. The Apache returned to a valley with a natural spring flowing into it from the south. Native Americans have inhabited this area for thousands of years, hunting the abundant game that grazed here. The grass grew as tall as a horse's belly and clear clean water from nearby springs flowed freely. The valley is shaped like a horseshoe, with the north opening to the high plateau. Hills rise to the west and east and a lava cliff can be seen to the south. There were other springs that dotted the base of the cliffs to the south of the valley. Native American ancestors left clear signs of their inhabitance and presence in the hills around Concho where pottery shards and arrowheads are sometimes found.

One of the boys captured eventually asked for permission to return to his family in Cubero. He had always remembered his Hispanic name—Manuel Antonio Candelaria. After the initial shock of seeing him again, his family welcomed him back, embraced him, and he was reintegrated into his Hispanic and Catholic community. Manuel Antonio, also known as "M.A." or "El Cautivo," later married Regina Baca and started a family. He brought that family to the area now known as Concho—along with a few hundred head of sheep and some sheepherders. They established a settlement in the 1860s in the place where he spent his youth.

Other men and families followed, and Concho grew to approximately 3,000 residents by the early 20th century. Concho was part of a larger sheepherding empire in a region that encompassed eastern Arizona and western New Mexico. As the town grew, a bank was established, and roads were built to facilitate the demands of a growing population and the needs of the sheepherding industry. During its heyday, Concho has its share of businesses, including rooms for rent for sheepherders, saloons, mercantile stores, stables, gas stations, and restaurants. Schools started at some homes where families were educated by their surrounding neighbors. Later, the Concho school was built, and generations of schoolchildren were educated there.

As their Nuevomexicano ancestors did, Concho families built their homes and places of worship out of adobe and dedicated their church to archangel San Rafael. A fiesta was held in his honor of

San Rafael and marked the harvest season in a community that proudly cultivated orchards, chile, and other agricultural goods. The local spring was held back by an earthen dam that was used to control water to the agricultural fields through ditches that were dug by hand or plowed with the help of horses. Every family had a cistern that they could use for washing clothes and cooking. The ditch ran year-round, and people used it as needed. During the planting season a *mayordomo* (steward or caretaker in Hispanic New Mexican tradition) was appointed to ensure that everyone got to use the water in an orderly manner and according to their needs. It was a yearly tradition each spring for men, women, and children to clean the ditches of the debris that might hold back the flow of water. Concho families decorated their homes with altars and their favorite saints. A morada was built for the Penitentes (religious brotherhood) who brought this tradition from New Mexico. Older men, or *hermanos*, participated in religious ceremonies held in the morada during the Lenten season. While this tradition has not continued, it is known that Concho was the farthest location west of New Mexico where the Penitentes migrated.

This book relates the story of that past through photographs—a community grounded in the faith and cultural practices of their Nuevomexicano ancestors, but one that has developed a unique identity and place-based consciousness from the time of its founding in the 1860s until today. By the 1930s and 1940s, Concho was becoming a different kind of community as men left to fight in World War II and more restrictive grazing rights gave way to a decline in sheepherding practices. Hispanics in Concho, however, continued to cultivate crops and grow spiritually through their participation in the San Rafael Church.

Many photographs contained in this book are from the private collections of Concho residents and were scanned and digitized as part of a University of Texas at Austin Center for Mexican American Studies/Voces Oral History Collaborative Fellowship that Vanessa Fonseca-Chávez received in 2023. Other photographs from the Library of Congress highlight the work of Russell Lee, who captured images of Concho's people, places, and landscapes in a position he held with the New Deal Farm Security Administration in the 1940s.

One

Las Familias

From the mid-1800s, the original sheepherders and employees of M.A. Candelaria sent word back to their families in New Mexico and an influx of settlers increased the region's population.

Some of the family surnames that originally came to Concho were Padilla, Archuleta, Durán, Romero, García, Archunde, Saiz, Sandoval, Pérez, Montoya, Chávez, Márquez, Ortega, Barreras, Baca, Saavedra, Sánchez, Tabor, López, Olivares, Ortiz, Peralta, Gallegos, Cipriano, Torrez, Azures, Tellez, Sena, Domínguez, and many more. The families that came to live in Concho were usually large families with several children and sometimes grandparents, aunts, and uncles accompanied them. They brought with them many skills they acquired in New Mexico. Family homes were made of adobe with lumber framing the doorways and windows. The floors of the homes were mostly dirt, although some families had wooden ones. Homes, stables, outhouses, and corrals had to be built, along with endless miles of fence.

The work was constant for parents. Children learned at a young age to do the tasks assigned to them. The older children helped keep the younger ones in check. Grandparents either lived by themselves close to the family or had a grandchild live with them as they aged. Sometimes, that child took on the grandparent's surname if it was different from their father's.

Even though families were large, many children died before reaching adulthood. In 1918, the Spanish Flu took the lives of many children. Childbirth often happened at home, with a midwife and sisters on hand during the delivery. Midwives also served as *curanderas*, or healers, and had great knowledge of local herbs and medicinal salves for several ailments. This tradition was often passed on to their daughters and is an important part of New Mexican Hispanic culture.

The photographs in this chapter contain images from many families and offer a glimpse into the lives of Concho's former and current residents. The map that begins the chapter offers readers a detailed and intimate look into the cartographies of these families—where they lived, who lived nearby, what businesses existed, and where families spent their leisure time in 1940 when the map was created. Many residents note that changes in grazing laws affected the sheepherding industry in the late 1930s and, beginning in the early 1940s, men were leaving Concho to fight in World War II. These shifts resulted in a need to create different economies and envision a different future for the town.

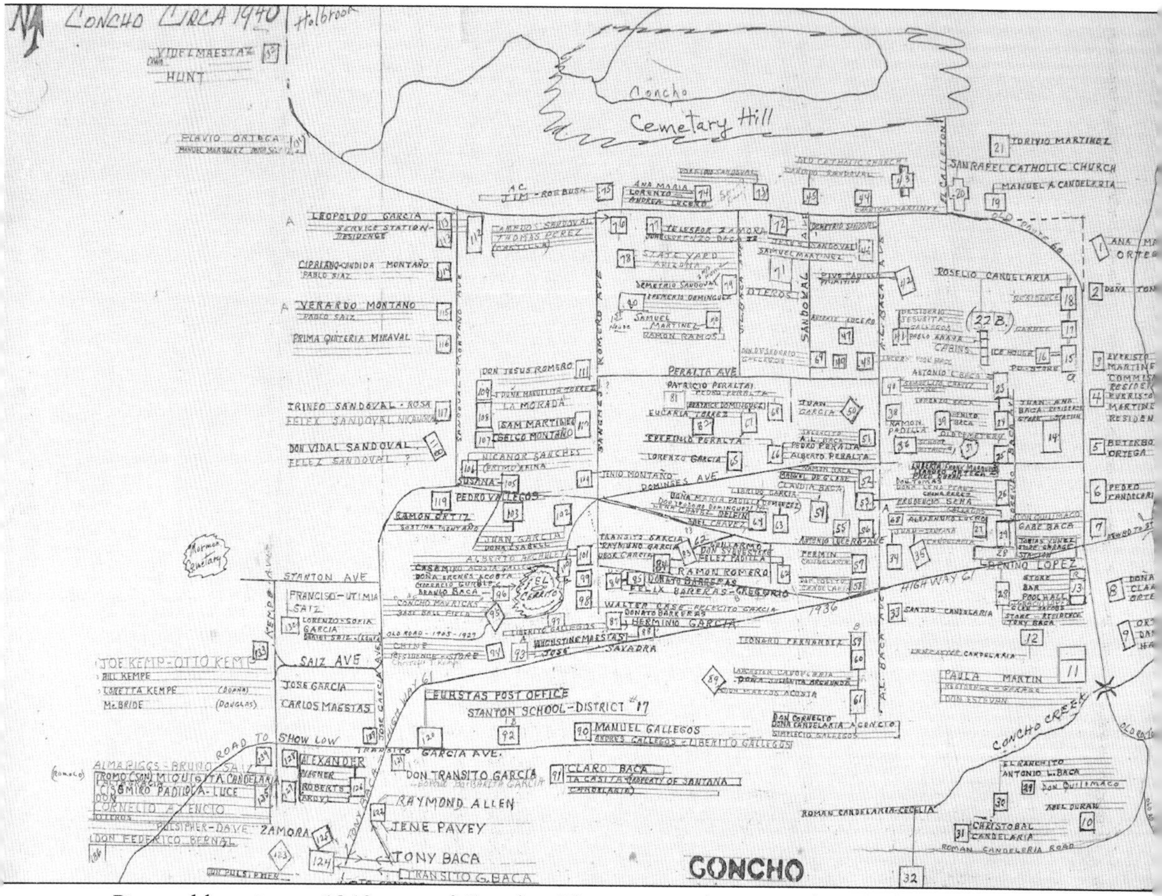

Pictured here is a c. 1940 map of Concho. The cartographer is unidentified, but the map shows where families lived and where ranches, businesses, and other institutions were located. The map was found among the personal possessions of Toney Baca following his death in the early 2000s. This map is an important community document, precisely because it contains information that is not available through other sources. The map not only indicates places and homes that belonged to Hispanic families, but it also shows where the Latter-day Saints communities resided and worked in Erastus, which was a short-lived settlement in Concho. In 1940, New Deal Federal Security Administration photographer Russell Lee captured many photographs of Concho. When viewed alongside the map, the photographs help to stitch together the town's history and the people who helped it grow. (Courtesy of Patrick Murphy.)

Rogerio "Roger" Candelaria and Dolores "Lola" (Baca) Candelaria are pictured here outside of a residence in 1922. Lola was originally from Quemado, New Mexico. They were married and later divorced. Roger passed away from alcoholism in his 50s, and Lola lived to be 103 years old. (Courtesy of Román Candelaria.)

From left to right are Herman Baca, Mary Ellen (McCullough) Candelaria, and Adelaida "Ida" Candelaria, who are standing outside of their home around 1930. Mary Ellen is the grandmother of Herman and Ida. (Courtesy of Román Candelaria.)

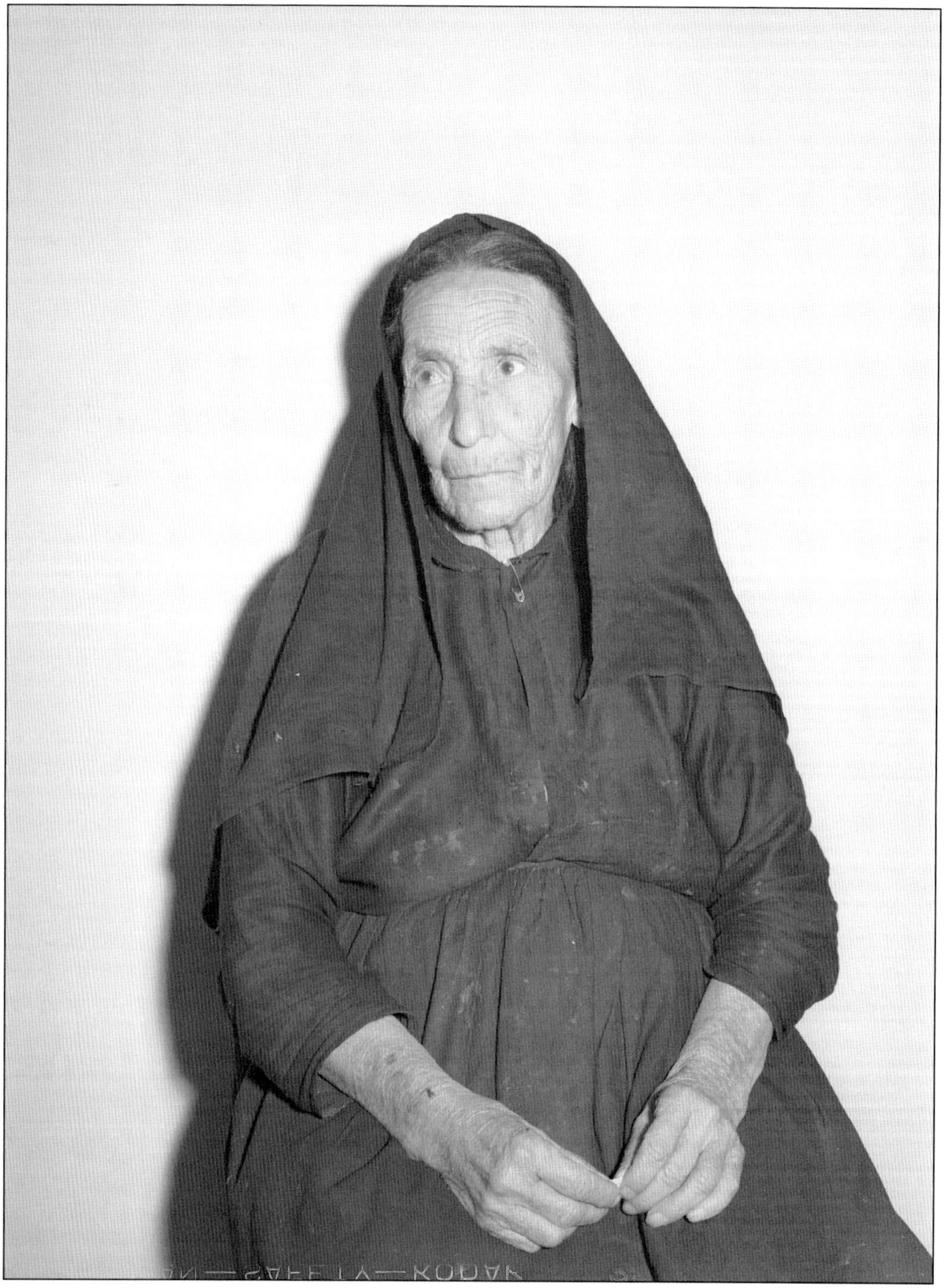

Felicita "Feliz" Padilla and her granddaughter Juanita (Romero) DeGlane once made mustard and oatmeal packs to cure Virginia Sánchez of pneumonia. They put her in a cold room and heated the packs to help save Virginia's life, despite the doctor telling them Virginia would not make it through the night. Feliz was one of a few women who knew the healing properties of local herbs. (Farm Security Administration/Office of War Information Black-and-White Negatives, Prints & Photographs Division, Library of Congress.)

From left to right, half-siblings Inez Candelaria and Evelyn Candelaria are seen here with their mother Anita (Gonzales) Candelaria and an unidentified boy on the Candelaria Ranch in Concho. (Courtesy of Román Candelaria.)

Isidro Baca is seen here on the Candelaria Ranch as a young boy. In the background are apple orchards, which were plentiful in Concho. Many ranches, including those located nearby and owned by Antonio L. Baca and Abel Durán, had orchards and/or animals. (Courtesy of Román Candelaria.)

Juanita (Romero) DeGlane stands in an adobe doorway in Concho, Arizona. Juanita was born in 1918 in Concho, six years after Arizona became a state. When she was two years old, her father left her mother, Feliz Padilla. Sarita (the eldest daughter) and Juanita lived with their grandmother Doña Feliz Romero. Juanita and Sarita's mother, Felicita, died when they were young. (Courtesy of Angela Perea-Murphy.)

Rafael "Ralph" Candelaria Jr., son of Pedro Román Candelaria and Anita (Gonzales) Candelaria is seated in a highchair celebrating his first birthday on the Candelaria Ranch. (Courtesy of Román Candelaria.)

Shown here is Pedro "Pete" Candelaria, the son of Rafael "Ralph" and Julia Candelaria, who was born in Concho in 1923. Other siblings that came later included Julia, Gabriel, Sofía, Elisa, and Cesario. (Courtesy of Román Candelaria.)

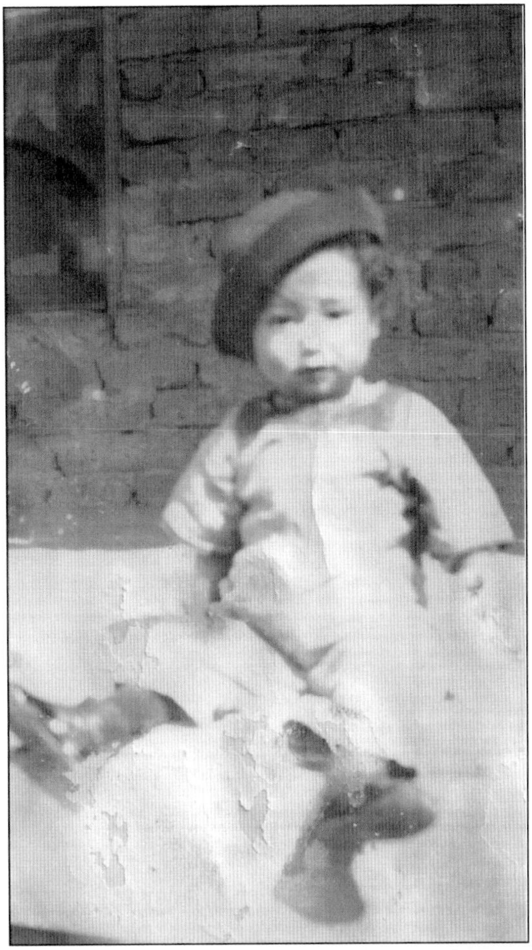

Pictured here are, from left to right, Tiodoro "Ted" López, Ida Candelaria, Lola López, unidentified, and Sofía López on the Candelaria Ranch. The ranch was a popular place for kids to gather and play. (Courtesy of Román Candelaria.)

Leopoldo "Leo" García, a former resident of Concho, sits near the remains of a house his family built in San Antonio, near Hunt, Arizona, likely located on Old Hunt Road, northwest of present-day Concho. His family lived in this house for a few years before moving to Concho. Leo was one year old when they moved from New Mexico to San Antonio. He was born in 1895 and passed away on January 23, 1985. (Courtesy of Angela Perea-Murphy.)

Leo and Barbara García pose for a photograph outside their home in front of the dining room window in Concho. (Courtesy of Angela Perea-Murphy.)

Seen here are Patrick "Pat" Murphy and Angela Perea-Murphy after they were married in Phoenix, Arizona, around 1967–1968. Pat was 24 years old, while Angela was 19 years old. They first met as students while enrolled at Phoenix College. (Courtesy of Patrick Murphy.)

Julia (left) and Emilia García, daughters of Reymundo García and Christina (Martínez) García, pose for a photograph outside of their home in Concho, Arizona. (Courtesy of Rudy Sánchez.)

Ramona Sánchez and Tony Allen Baca are at a home in Phoenix, Arizona. Ramona is the granddaughter of Reymundo García and Christina (Martínez) García and Tony Allen is the son of Toney Baca and Pauline Baca. Many families migrated to the Phoenix area after World War II. (Courtesy of Rudy Sánchez.)

Leo García is seated outside of his home in Concho with his dog. In the background is an outdoor altar, dedicated to a Catholic Marian image. It was common for community members to have religious imagery inside and outside of their homes. (Courtesy of Angela Perea-Murphy.)

Barbara García (left) stands next to Marguerite DeVille outside of the García home in Concho around 1964. Many children arrived in Concho and were placed in the care of the Garcías, a foster family. (Courtesy of Angela Perea-Murphy.)

From left to right, Linda Perea, Alex Perea, and Angela Perea stand in their front yard in Concho during the fall of 1967. (Courtesy of Angela Perea-Murphy.)

From left to right, Darlene Nosie, Berdina Nosie, and Marilyn Nosie stand together in front of the home of Barbara and Leo García. They were among many children who were fostered by the García family. (Courtesy of Angela Perea-Murphy.)

Juan Candelaria is seen here, photographed in October 1940 in Concho. The Candelaria family is one of the first families to arrive in Concho to work as sheepherders. Of the families and individuals who were photographed by Russell Lee as part of the New Deal Farm Security Administration, only the Candelaria family is noted by name. (Farm Security Administration/Office of War Information Black-and-White Negatives, Prints & Photographs Division, Library of Congress.)

Cecilia (Chávez) Candelaria stands outside her home in Concho around 1915–1920. She is dressed in a style typical of the time period, and likely for a special occasion. Her outfit stands in stark contrast to the adobe wall seen behind her. (Courtesy of Hope MacMonagle.)

Roger Candelaria Jr. (left) is seen here with his cousin Isidro López, son of Patricia López. In the background is a typical Concho high desert landscape, dotted with short grass, piñon, and juniper trees. (Courtesy of Román Candelaria.)

Pedro Román Candelaria and his first wife, Cecilia (Chávez) Candelaria, stand alongside his brother Roger Candelaria (left to right). Pedro Román was 22 years old, and Cecilia was 15 when they were married. (Courtesy of Román Candelaria.)

Pictured are, from left to right, Johnny López Jr., Pedro Román Candelaria, and Isauro López. The López boys were sons of Patricia López. Román Candelaria shared that after Patricia passed away in the 1930s, Pedro Román helped raise them on the Candelaria Ranch. (Courtesy of Román Candelaria.)

From left to right, Julia Nuañez, Pedro Román Candelaria, and Lucinda "Cinda" (Fernández) Padilla pose for a photograph. Cinda was married to Porfie Padilla. (Courtesy of Hope MacMonagle.)

Inez Candelaria is seen here in front of the family home standing near her bicycle around 1950. (Courtesy of Román Candelaria.)

Evelyn Candelaria rides a pony named Chubby at the Candelaria Ranch. It was not uncommon for children to become attached to the animals they helped to raise on the ranch. In the background is likely a water tank, which was generally used to hold drinking water or water for household use. (Courtesy of Román Candelaria.)

Pictured from left to right in their Sunday best are Santana Candelaria and Patricia Candelaria, daughters of Pedro Candelaria and Mary Ellen (McCullough) Candelaria. (Courtesy of Román Candelaria.)

Dodie Baca is seen here at her family home in Holbrook, Arizona. She is the fourth child of Inez and Filo Baca. (Courtesy of Román Candelaria.)

Pedro Román Candelaria (left) sits next to his grandmother Miquelita Candelaria around 1909. This photograph is the oldest one that appears in this book. (Courtesy of Román Candelaria.)

From left to right, sisters Santana Candelaria and Patricia Candelaria stand together with their brother Pedro Román Candelaria and his wife, Cecilia (Chávez) Candelaria, near the front porch of a residence. (Courtesy of Román Candelaria.)

An unidentified family is seen here in their home in Concho in October 1940. On the wall behind the family are family photographs and a calendar from Juan Candelaria and Son Mercantile Company, a local business in Concho. (Farm Security Administration/Office of War Information Black-and-White Negatives, Prints & Photographs Division, Library of Congress.)

Gabriel "Gabe" Baca and Ida (Candelaria) Baca are pictured here in Concho around the time they were married in 1936. (Courtesy of Román Candelaria.)

Gabe Baca (left) is seen here at the dinner table with his family in Concho around 1967. Around the time this photo was taken, Gabe was growing cucumbers in Concho and transporting them to Snowflake, Arizona. The cucumbers eventually made their way to Phoenix to the Arnold Pickle & Olive Company, which was founded in 1909. (Courtesy of Hope MacMonagle.)

Regina Baca (right) is with her daughter Victoria at their home in Santa Ana, California, in May 1967. Regina is one of 10 children of Gabe Baca and Ida (Candelaria) Baca. (Courtesy of Regina (Baca) Shaver.)

From left to right, Maximiliano "Max" Baca, Hope Baca, and Mark Baca are standing near the front door of their home in Concho in 1967. These siblings are three of Gabe Baca and Ida (Candelaria) Baca's 10 children. (Courtesy of Hope MacMonagle.)

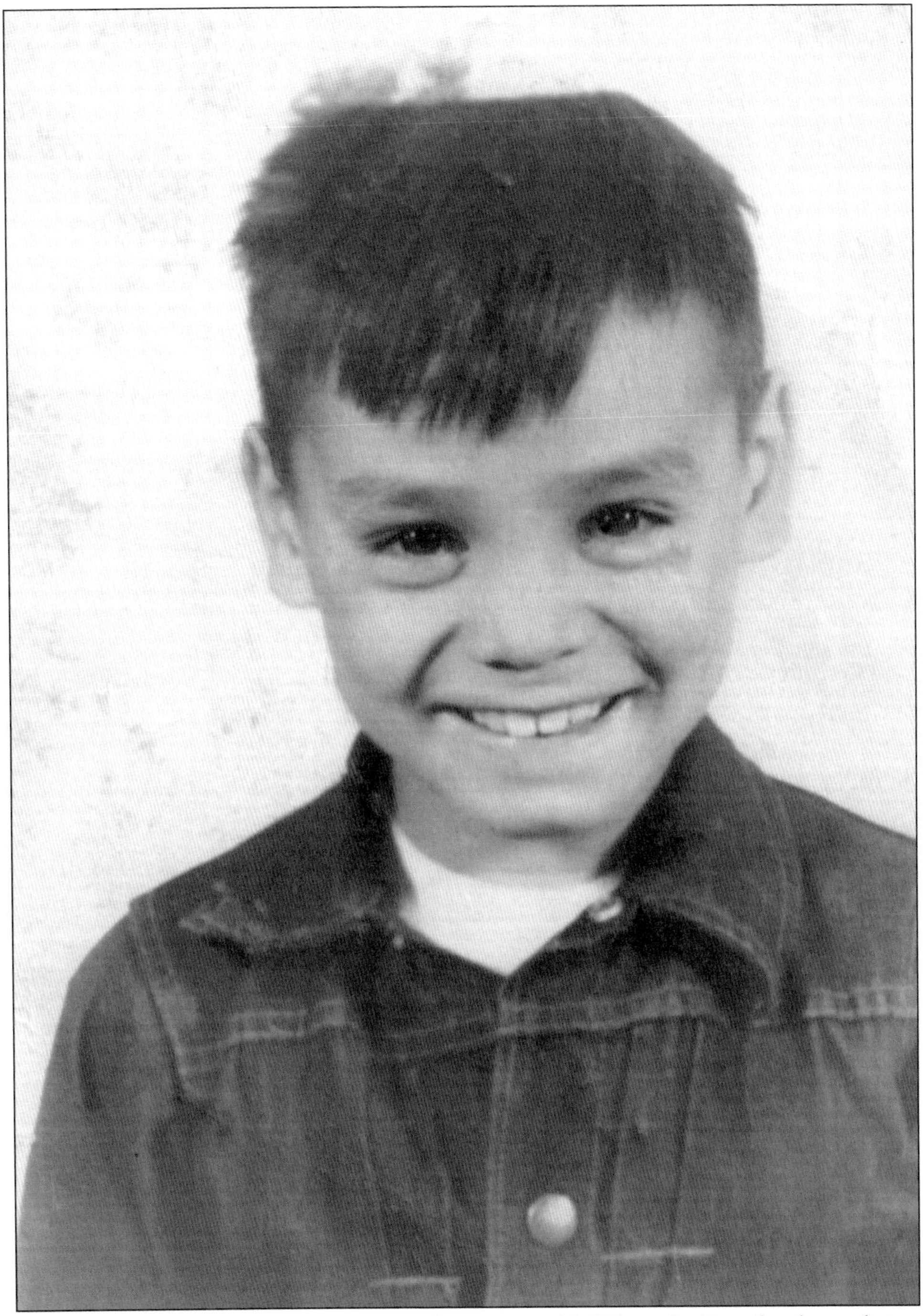

Pictured here is Gabriel Baca at approximately six years old. When the Baca family was living in Tempe, Arizona, they were involved in a train collision that resulted in Gabriel's death at the age of ten years old. Three of his siblings were injured as well. The incident was covered in the *Arizona Republic* on Friday, October 19, 1951, in an article titled "Train Injures Tempe Family." In 1954, the *Arizona Republic* reported that Gabriel's parents, Gabe Baca and Ida (Candelaria) Baca, won $25,000 in a settlement with the Southern Pacific Co. (Courtesy of Regina (Baca) Shaver.)

From left to right, siblings Hope Baca, Max Baca, and Gabriella "Gabie" Baca are photographed as young children in Tempe, Arizona, in 1956. (Courtesy of Hope MacMonagle.)

Pictured here at their home in Tempe, Arizona, in 1956 are, from left to right, siblings Hope Baca, Carmen Baca, and Gabie Baca. (Courtesy of Hope MacMonagle.)

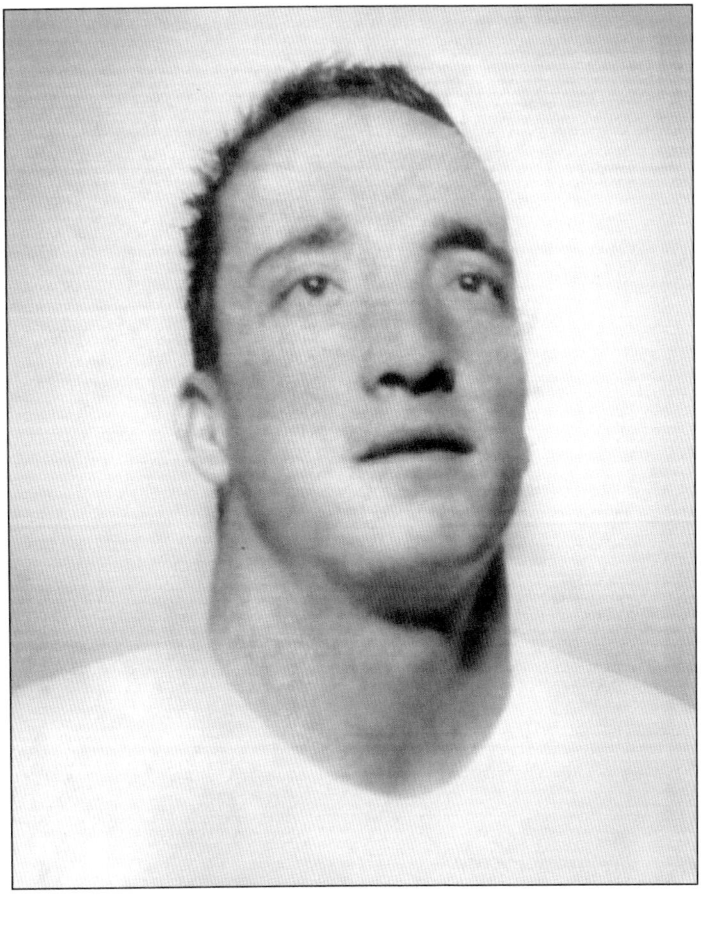

Charlie Durán is photographed here for Golden Gloves Boxing. Starting in 1923, Golden Gloves of America Inc. provided opportunities for young men to gain skills in the boxing arena and to develop future talent. (Courtesy of Mishaela Durán.)

Pictured here is the home of Frank Márquez and Cecilia (Durán) Márquez in October 1940. The adobe home was located across the highway from the Durán Ranch, and it was located close to the Concho school. Among his many occupations, Frank was a business owner in Concho and lived his whole life there. He passed away at the age of 49 in 1968. Cecilia later moved to Phoenix and lived until the age of 81, passing away in 1998. (Farm Security Administration/Office of War Information Black-and-White Negatives, Prints & Photographs Division, Library of Congress.)

Phillip (García) Ulibarrí (left) and his youngest brother Filomeno (García) Ulibarrí Jr. are seen here in 1965. The backside of the photograph reads, "To Grandma, From Phillip and Meno." Filomeno grew up in St. Johns but has family roots in Concho. He and his wife, Juanita (Soto) Ulibarrí, moved to Concho in the early 2000s and resided on his grandfather's land. Filomeno passed away in 2023 at his home in Concho. (Courtesy of Juanita (Soto) Ulibarrí.)

Juanita (Soto) Ulibarrí is pictured here in a school photograph wearing a cross necklace. Juanita was raised in Holbrook and later met and married Filomeno (García) Ulibarrí Jr. They raised their family in Flagstaff and moved to Concho, where his grandfather was from. (Courtesy of Juanita (Soto) Ulibarrí.)

Juanita (Soto) Ulibarrí's grandmother, Vicenta (Serna) González, mother of Veneranda (Gurule) Soto, stands in her yard wearing an apron. This photograph was taken in February 1960 in Holbrook, Arizona. (Courtesy of Juanita (Soto) Ulibarrí.)

A picture of Arthur "Art" Salas in October 1953, addressed to his aunt and uncle. On the back of the photograph is "To my uncle and auntie Charlie and Sally Love, Artie." (Courtesy of Art Salas.)

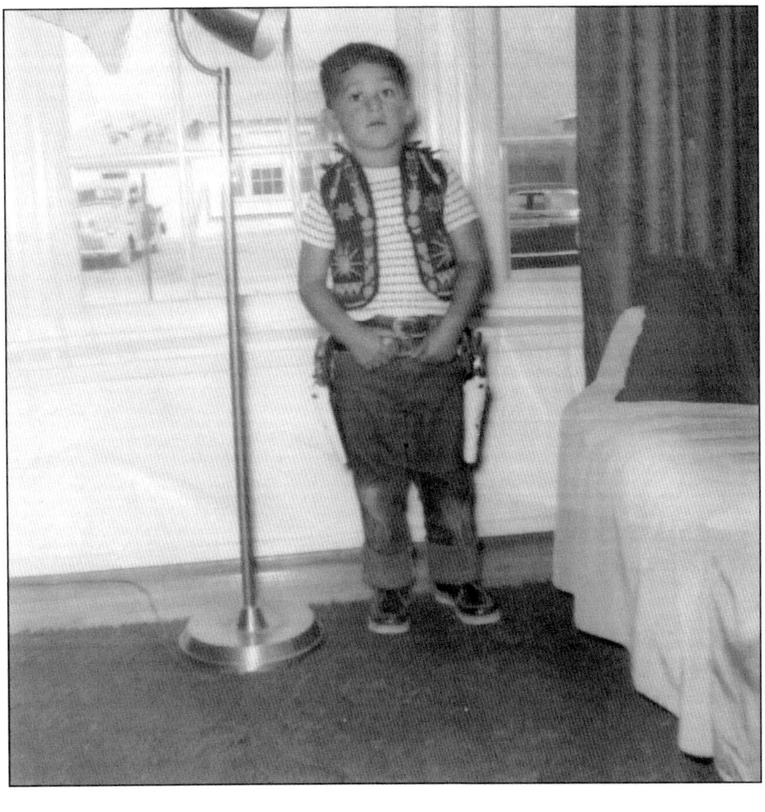

Art Salas is seen here during Christmastime in Pico Rivera, California in 1952. Art was three years old. His mother, Lorraine (Peralta Sandoval) Salas, was born in Concho, Arizona. (Courtesy of Art Salas.)

From left to right, Bill Salas, Art Salas, and Lorraine (Peralta Sandoval) Salas pose for a family photograph on Easter in Pico Rivera, California, in 1952. (Courtesy of Art Salas.)

Seen here is Jesús María Sandoval (left), ancestor of Art Salas, with an unidentified man. The Sandoval family has a dedicated section of the Concho Catholic Cemetery for their family, which has been in Concho for many generations. (Courtesy of Art Salas.)

Two

LIVELIHOODS

M.A. Candelaria came to northeastern Arizona because water was accessible and grazing land for sheep was abundant. Domestic sheep were first brought by the conquistadores from Spain. Concho men worked as sheepherders and walked many miles guiding the flocks of sheep, guarding them against wild animals and thieves. In the late 1800s, Concho had become one of the largest sheep and wool-raising centers in the US Southwest, along with many rural communities in northwestern New Mexico. The sheep owners employed maids, nannies, gardeners, and tutors for their children. Those employed were usually the wives and children of the sheepherders. It would not be surprising at that time to see 100,000 head of sheep grazing in the hills around Concho. New Mexican Hispanic and Indigenous peoples adopted cultural practices from sheep, including the production of textile arts such as colchas and weavings.

Established in 1902 as the first bank in the county, the Apache County Bank served the Concho community as well as held accounts from nearby towns such as St. Johns, Springerville, and Holbrook. Many of the stockholders were descendants of M.A. Candelaria. The presence of a bank in Concho speaks to the thriving businesses and financial transactions that were necessary to ensure that this growing town was supported. Many businesses sprung up as the town grew, including beauty shops, garages, and mercantile stores, among others. E.M. Deglane (1981) dedicates Chapter 8 of his book to Early Concho Merchants.

The families of Concho worked hard to survive. The fall was the time of harvest and food had to be preserved for the winter. This included hours of husking corn, stringing chilies, and drying fruits and vegetables. Summer and fall months were spent gathering wood to use in the woodstoves for warmth and for cooking in the colder months. Livestock had to be fed and kept safe throughout the winter. In the late fall, butchering was done. This was usually a social event where families and neighbors assisted. Everyone went home with a piece of meat and a hearty meal under their belt, which was prepared by the women. Vegetables were stored in *a soterrano* (cellar) to keep them from going bad or freezing. Spring brought with it new jobs, including plowing the fields and getting them ready for planting. Families cleaned ditches to ensure that water would run properly, and chicken coops, pig pens, and barns would be readied to welcome newborn animals.

The Concho sign was located on the old road from St. Johns to Concho. The Doña Clara Ortega house and the Ortega Dance Hall are seen, with the Texaco and Apache Café located across the street. This business was operated by the López family. (Farm Security Administration/Office of War Information Black-and-White Negatives, Prints & Photographs Division, Library of Congress.)

The homestead of Pedro Román Candelaria is seen here in October 1940. He is standing behind the wagon, and there are chickens and ducks scattered nearby. Near the side of the home is an unidentified man crouched down and gazing toward the camera. This home is still standing today and has been remodeled. (Farm Security Administration/Office of War Information Black-and-White Negatives, Prints & Photographs Division, Library of Congress.)

Shown here is the view from the front yard of a residential home. The map at the beginning of Chapter One suggests it may be the home of Beterbo "B.D." Ortega. Across the street is the Santa Anita Store, which was owned by J.D. Baca. (Farm Security Administration/Office of War Information Black-and-White Negatives, Prints & Photographs Division, Library of Congress.)

The Santa Anita Store was owned by J.D. Baca, a local merchant, and was located on the main street in Concho near other businesses. It was later owned by A.C. Roebush. The store had a service station out front and, in contrast to other businesses photographed by Russell Lee in October 1940, it appeared to be in better condition. (Farm Security Administration/Office of War Information Black-and-White Negatives, Prints & Photographs Division, Library of Congress.)

Shown here is Hotel Martínez, owned by Evaristo Martínez and located in Concho. Rooms and meals were offered at the hotel. The sign on a nearby storefront reads, "Chesterfields Satisfy," which was an ad for a popular cigarette brand in the 1940s. A young woman is also seen, holding hands with a child as they approach the storefront. (Farm Security Administration/Office of War Information Black-and-White Negatives, Prints & Photographs Division, Library of Congress.)

Seen here is the main street in Concho in October 1940. This building held businesses including a garage, post office, mercantile store, and a service station. Next to it is the residence of Rosalío Candelaria, son of M.A. Candelaria and Regina (Baca) Candelaria. (Farm Security Administration/Office of War Information Black-and-White Negatives, Prints & Photographs Division, Library of Congress.)

Seven men are facing toward the camera for a photograph. In the front is Leo García, holding a leash with a dog; from left to right in the second row are Cándido Sandoval, Rosalío Candelaria, three unidentified men, and Bernardo Montaño. They all stand in front of the Concho Post Office around 1928. García worked as a mail carrier for some time and was a lifelong resident of Concho, much like other men photographed here. As can be seen from the photograph on the previous page, the building received a facelift by 1940 and was painted white with new signage. (Courtesy of Angela Perea-Murphy.)

Fidel Gonzales and Dorothy (Lewis) Gonzales's children, from left to right, Gloria, Linda, and Marty are at the Gonzales Beauty Shop in Concho. Fidel was the youngest brother of Anita (Gonzales) Candelaria. Fidel worked as a barber at the beauty shop, and his family often assisted with the business. The photograph is festive in nature, with the Gonzales children donning big grins, and with Fidel holding two maracas. (Courtesy of Román Candelaria.)

Postmaster Mónico Candelaria, son of Rosalío Candelaria, is working at the post office located inside his father's general store on main street in Concho, located just north of the Santa Anita Store that was run by J.D. Baca. Mónico left Concho to serve in World War II, and by the 1950s, the family had moved to Albuquerque, New Mexico. (Farm Security Administration/Office of War Information Black-and-White Negatives, Prints & Photographs Division, Library of Congress.)

A woman is seen here weighing produce at a local store in October 1940. Also in the photograph is a small chile ristra hanging behind her and a display for Holsum Bread, which could be purchased at the store. A variety of dry goods and seasonal foods were available at the general store. (Farm Security Administration/Office of War Information Black-and-White Negatives, Prints & Photographs Division, Library of Congress.)

A former tourist court is seen here. Tourist courts provided a place for travelers to stay, with adjacent covered and enclosed parking for their vehicles. The tourist court seen here is not being used for its original purpose. Instead, it had been converted into a barn and appears to be storing corn stalks. (Farm Security Administration/Office of War Information Black-and-White Negatives, Prints & Photographs Division, Library of Congress.)

Roger Candelaria and Lola (Baca) Candelaria stand at a service station gas pump, with the insignia of Magnolia Gasoline on top. This photograph was taken in 1922, when Lola was pregnant with their first child, Roger. (Courtesy of Román Candelaria.)

An unidentified woman (left) stands next to Pedro Román Candelaria at a gas pump in Concho around 1922. (Courtesy of Román Candelaria.)

Reymundo García is at work at the service station located at the Candelaria General Store in Concho in the early 1920s. The store was located at the present-day Old Concho Community Center. (Courtesy of Rudy Sánchez.)

Reymundo García and Christina (Martínez) García are seen here with their grandson at their establishment, El Concho Café, located at 1654 W. Washington Street in Phoenix, Arizona. The couple moved from Concho to Phoenix in 1939 and opened the café, serving Spanish food like "Inchildads [*sic*]," "Tomales [*sic*]," and "Tacos," as indicated on their business card. Reymundo was born in 1903 in Concho to Tránsito J. García and Seferina García. (Courtesy of Rudy Sánchez.)

Pedro Román Candelaria is pictured with his daughter Ida Candelaria and their sheep on the family ranch. Ida was the only child born of Pedro Román and Cecilia (Chávez) Candelaria. Pedro Román took over the ranch in 1912, the same year Arizona was granted statehood. His father, Pedro Antonio Candelaria, purchased the ranch in 1896. (Courtesy of Román Candelaria.)

Two Candelaria brothers are seen here with their dog, with a typical Concho landscape in the background, taken in October 1940. (Farm Security Administration/Office of War Information Black-and-White Negatives, Prints & Photographs Division, Library of Congress.)

A flock of sheep is seen here grazing in Concho. Sheepherding was the primary economy in the late 19th and early 20th centuries in this area, and many Concho men worked in the industry. In 1936, the Taylor Grazing Act was established, which provided stricter oversight of public grazing lands. (Farm Security Administration/Office of War Information Black-and-White Negatives, Prints & Photographs Division, Library of Congress.)

Cristóbal Candelaria and Pedro Román Candelaria are pictured on horseback in 1932. When families shifted from raising sheep to raising cattle, horses became an increasingly important part of their lives. Many ranchers utilized horses to help wrangle cattle and to reach parts of the ranch that were not as easily accessible by other means. (Courtesy of Román Candelaria.)

Román Candelaria and his father, Pedro Román Candelaria, pose for a photograph at their ranch in Concho around 1958. (Courtesy of Román Candelaria.)

Two bulls are seen here, across the lake on the Candelaria Ranch. The lake was created from a spring at the Snake Ranch and was used for field irrigation and as a water source for animals. (Courtesy of Román Candelaria.)

Pictured here is Pinto the horse on the Candelaria Ranch. Pinto likely got his name because he resembles the coloring of a pinto bean. Horses were essential to ranch life in Concho. (Courtesy of Román Candelaria.)

From left to right, Jim Santiago Márquez, Jimmy García, Pedro Román Candelaria, and Toney Baca are at a reunion in Concho. Jim was later a chef at one of the resorts at the Grand Canyon. He was born in 1915 and passed away in 1976. Family reunions were common, and families often cooked for many individuals who came from afar to attend. Many families used pit barbecues to cook the meat and beans for gatherings. This tradition continues today with the Padilla family, who cooks the meat for the annual San Rafael Catholic Church Fiesta. (Courtesy of Rudy Sánchez.)

From left to right, Román Candelaria, Leo Archuleta, and Pedro Román Candelaria assist with cattle branding around 1960. Each rancher had a unique brand that was utilized to mark their cattle and to keep thieves away. If cattle were found on nearby ranches, they could be identified easily by the rancher who owned them and returned. (Courtesy of Román Candelaria.)

From left to right, an unidentified man and an unidentified woman assist Pedro Román Candelaria as they butcher a hog, around 1930. (Courtesy of Román Candelaria.)

Best friends Manuel Gallegos (left) and Pedro Román Candelaria are seen here on a hunt near Concho in about 1927. (Courtesy of Román Candelaria.)

Lee "Pinocho" López, a Concho resident, stands next to a mountain lion that his father, Fermín López, killed after finding it in a tree in his orchard. In the early days of Concho, many families herded sheep, and mountain lions posed a threat to the flocks. By the 1940s, the number of sheep had been significantly reduced in the region, and cattle ranching gained popularity over sheepherding. (Courtesy of Angela Perea-Murphy.)

Max Baca (left) and Phillip Baca stand in front of heavy machinery. The photograph was taken when they were staying with Román Candelaria and Bertha Candelaria in Sanders, Arizona. (Courtesy of Román Candelaria.)

Evelyn Candelaria, daughter of Pedro Román Candelaria and Anita (Gonzales) Candelaria, is operating heavy machinery on the Candelaria Ranch in 1956. (Courtesy of Román Candelaria.)

Pedro Román Candelaria's 1955 Ford is parked in front of the bee boxes and orchards. The bee boxes were located on the side of the hill next to the Candelaria family home. Courthouse representative Noah Connely's son raised bees, just as Pedro Román did. (Courtesy of Román Candelaria.)

Román Candelaria (left) and Albert Archuleta stand in front of a brand-new Ford pickup in the summer of 1955. (Courtesy of Román Candelaria.)

Pedro Román Candelaria (left) poses next to the first John Deere tractor that came to Concho. An unidentified man is seated behind the wheel. (Courtesy of Román Candelaria.)

A cornfield is seen here following a flood, resulting from a dam break, on the Candelaria Ranch, Residents recall that the dam break caused fish to be deposited across the fields of many ranches in the area. The corn crop was more bountiful than normal due to the increased water in the fields. Ida Candelaria (in front) is seated on the back of the wagon, with two unidentified individuals. (Courtesy of Hope MacMonagle.)

Benito Gonzales is listed in the 1940 US Federal Census as a hired hand and lodger. He assisted the Pedro Román Candelaria family on the ranch. There were many men who found work on ranches in the Concho area. Ranching families have lived in this area for many years and many families continue to operate ranches, albeit on a smaller scale than their ancestors once did. (Courtesy of Román Candelaria.)

Angela Perea was photographed at around 12 or 13 years old in front of a cornfield with her García family in 1961. The family had a lot of crops and often worked in the fields. Barbara García, Perea's foster mom, was 18 when she married Leo, who was 45 years old at the time. The García family did not have any biological kids but fostered many children in Concho, and adopted one child named Stephen Gregory García. Pictured are, from left to right, Angela Perea, Linda Perea, Mary Perea, Adolph Perea, Leo García, and Barbara García. (Courtesy of Angela Perea-Murphy.)

An adobe home is pictured here where chile ristras are hanging on each external wall. In the background is the Concho School. When chile is fresh, it is green and produces a unique flavor and texture. As green chile matures, it turns red and takes on a different flavor profile. To utilize red chile, it must be first dried. Families would gather together to create ristras so that the red chile could dry completely before storing. (Farm Security Administration/Office of War Information Black-and-White Negatives, Prints & Photographs Division, Library of Congress.)

Pedro Román Candelaria sits on a bench shucking corn, one of the many crops that families in Concho grew. Corn could be dried in a *horno*, or outdoor oven, to make *chicos* (dried corn) for the winter, providing a food source in colder months. The husks could be cleaned and dried to make tamales or could be used as feed for animals. (Farm Security Administration/Office of War Information Black-and-White Negatives, Prints & Photographs Division, Library of Congress.)

A worker collects and sorts chile peppers that were grown in Concho in 1940. Concho chile has been grown for many generations in Concho. Chile grows well in Concho because the climate is like that of New Mexico. While some residents say that Concho has its own heirloom chile, others say their chile is likely a variation of the New Mexican variety. In a 2003 newspaper article titled "The Last Concho Chili Farm," Carroll Cox writes that Concho residents save chile seeds each season, just as their ancestors did since they arrived in Concho. (Farm Security Administration/Office of War Information Black-and-White Negatives, Prints & Photographs Division, Library of Congress.)

A Concho elder is seen here proudly displaying chile ristras. When the green chile turned red (a more mature form), it would be strung up and hung to form ristras. This would dry out the chile to be used as either decoration or as a food source. Dried red chile could be hydrated and pulverized to turn into a red sauce, or the dried pods could be turned into a powder to then make a sauce. Chile remains a staple of many Concho households and is incorporated into almost every meal. (Farm Security Administration/Office of War Information Black-and-White Negatives, Prints & Photographs Division, Library of Congress.)

A group of men are seen here constructing a bridge, using a horse-drawn tiller and pickaxes to break up the dirt. As more families moved to Concho and ranches, businesses, schools, and religious institutions were established, more infrastructure was needed to sustain them. (Farm Security Administration/Office of War Information Black-and-White Negatives, Prints & Photographs Division, Library of Congress.)

A man is seen here assisting with the construction of the Concho Dam around 1923–1927. The dam was a necessity to ensure that water was available and utilized efficiently for Concho residents, businesses, and ranches. (Courtesy of Román Candelaria.)

A group of families gather here for a photograph. On the left holding a young child is Ralph Candelaria, and to his right is Pete Domínguez. The others are unidentified. (Courtesy of Román Candelaria.)

Seen here is a photograph of men working in a lumber yard. Cousins Regina Baca and Evelyn Candelaria often spent their summers in the lumber yards. Regina's father, Gabe Baca, worked in this industry for many years, as did other Concho men. (Courtesy of Regina (Baca) Shaver.)

An unidentified woman sits at her dining room table in her home sorting beans. Many Concho families had gardens where they planted pinto beans. Beans could also be purchased in bulk from the general stores where dry goods were sold. Beans and chile were and continue to be a staple in the homes of many Concho families. Libor and Domitilia "Tillie" García's son, Greg García, had a pinto bean field where they used to grow chile. (Farm Security Administration/Office of War Information Black-and-White Negatives, Prints & Photographs Division, Library of Congress.)

An unidentified woman stands at her dining room table working with dried meat, gourds, pumpkins, and canned fruit, including peaches. It was common during the fall harvest to prepare food to last through the winter season. Food could be dried or canned and it was often stored in a *soterrano*, or basement cellar. (Farm Security Administration/Office of War Information Black-and-White Negatives, Prints & Photographs Division, Library of Congress.)

Three

Church, School, and Military

From the very beginning, Concho was Catholic. Although there was not a priest in the area, families observed the feast days of saints and holy days of obligation. They also would participate in a pilgrimage to visit the Santo Niño de Atocha at Zuni Pueblo, one of the most frequented pilgrimage sites in northwestern New Mexico. The first Catholic church in Concho burned down around the 1930s, according to oral history interviews with Concho residents. Art Salas's ancestors José Cándido Sandoval and Elesea Sandoval purchased a nearby building previously owned by Christopher J. Kempe. It was donated by the Sandoval family for the purpose of constructing the present-day San Rafael Catholic Church.

E.M. DeGlane, in 1981, wrote that the early years of schooling in Concho consisted of parents educating their children in their homes primarily in Spanish. In some cases, more wealthy families could afford tutors. At the Snake Ranch, the Ortega family started a school with a teacher who came from New Mexico. It was not common, however, for children to attend past primary grades because there was work to do at home to help the family. According to DeGlane, there were many different buildings over time that housed the school. The school building that most people remember served children from 1920 until the 1980s. It had two rooms: one dedicated to first through fourth-grade instruction, and another dedicated to fifth through eighth grade. The old school was eventually sold to the Diocese of Gallup and used as a historical museum until it burned down.

Concho has long considered itself a patriotic town. Some of its founders served in the American Civil War. There were many men in Concho who fought in World War I, and it seemed that almost every man in town enlisted to serve in World War II. Toney Baca, son of Antonio and Elviria García Baca, enlisted in September 1941, and was one of the first to join the war efforts. After the war was declared by the United States on December 7, 1941, every eligible young man— and some not so eligible and too young— tried to enlist. They often communicated with family members by sending personal letters, many of which were published in the local newspapers. To this day, the military and veteran community in Concho is strong.

Seen here is the interior of the San Rafael Catholic Church in 1931. There was a wood-burning stove and a choir loft that no longer exists in the present-day church. The front altar has statues of Our Lady of Guadalupe, San Rafael, and St. Anthony. Other saints adorn the church. The old benches have since been removed, and a gas stove was installed in 1955 to replace the wood-burning stove. Following Vatican II in the late 1960s, all saints and altars in the church were stripped. According to residents, the altar in the back of the church was burned by the resident priest in the late 1960s and early 1970s. The altar screen was then removed, and wood paneling was installed by the Padilla family. The old stations of the cross are still there, which are original to the church that was across the road from the present-day San Rafael Catholic Church. (Courtesy of Angela Perea-Murphy.)

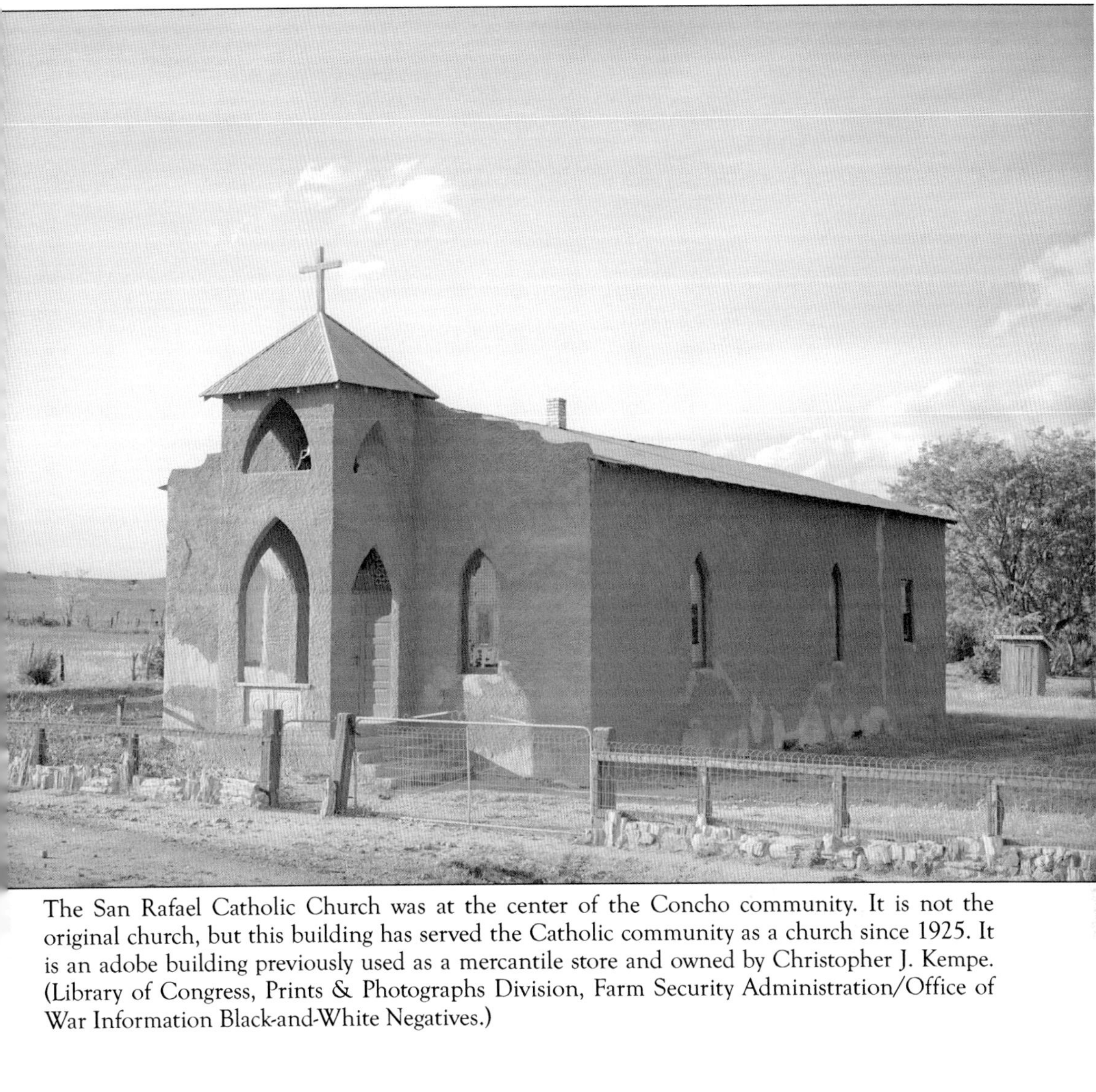

The San Rafael Catholic Church was at the center of the Concho community. It is not the original church, but this building has served the Catholic community as a church since 1925. It is an adobe building previously used as a mercantile store and owned by Christopher J. Kempe. (Library of Congress, Prints & Photographs Division, Farm Security Administration/Office of War Information Black-and-White Negatives.)

Regina Peralta García (daughter of Pablo Peralta and María Matrónica Baca) is seen outside with her four kids—Donna, Martha, Tránsito, and Paul—(left to right) as they are heading to church. Children rarely dressed up, except to attend church or church functions. Regina was married to Simplicio García, who was raised by his uncle Juan Márquez. At times, Simplicio adopted the surname Márquez, or Marqués. (Courtesy of Rudy Sánchez.)

From left to right, Freddie (García) Ulibarrí, Filomeno (García) Ulibarrí Jr., and Chris (García) Ulibarrí pose for a photograph at their First Holy Communion. Each of them holds a prayer book, a candle, and a rosary. (Courtesy of Juanita (Soto) Ulibarrí.)

Seen here is a First Holy Communion group at San Rafael Catholic Church in 1956. Pictured from left to right are Fr. Harry Morgan, Alex Padilla, Anna Maestas, Yvonne DeGlane, Angela Perea, Angie Barreras, Patsy Márquez, Paula Padilla, Davey García, and Sofía García. (Courtesy of Angela Perea-Murphy.)

Inez Candelaria, daughter of Pedro Román Candelaria and Anita (Gonzales) Candelaria, holds a rosary and a prayer card in a photograph for her First Holy Communion. (Courtesy of Román Candelaria.)

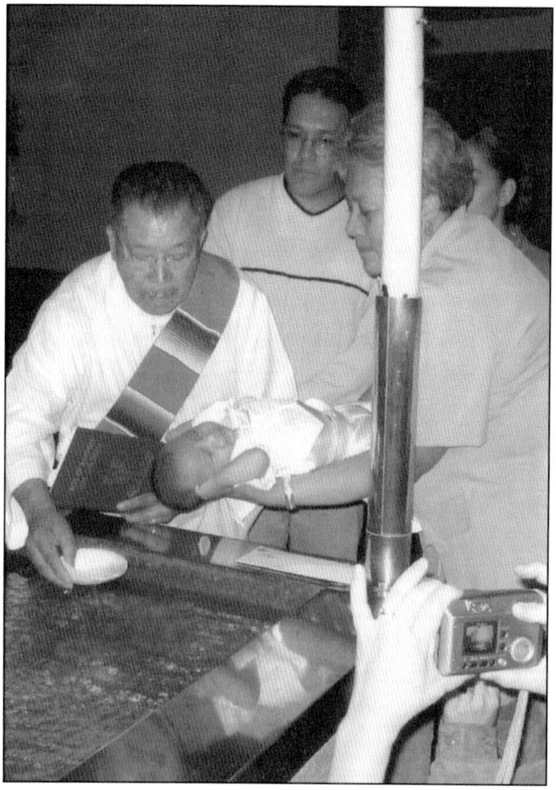

Deacon Filomeno (García) Ulibarrí Jr. (left) is baptizing his grandson, Isidro. Behind him is his son, Filomeno. Deacon Filomeno was ordained in 1999, and for 11 years, he served the parishes of St. John the Baptist and San Rafael in St. Johns and Concho, respectively. (Courtesy of Juanita (Soto) Ulibarrí.)

Seen here is Kenneth Durán dressed up for his First Holy Communion at San Rafael Catholic Church in 1967. Kenneth was the grandson of Concho residents Abrán (Chávez) Durán and Agueda "Aggie" (Gonzales) Durán and the son of Charlie (Gonzales) Durán and Angelina "Angie" (Baca) Durán. Fr. Alfred Tachías, who was born in Cabezón, New Mexico, was the priest at San Rafael during this time. Father Tachías spent his entire career working for the Diocese of Gallup, where he was ordained as a priest in 1959. (Courtesy of Mishaela Durán.)

Lorraine (Peralta Sandoval) Salas, mother of Art Salas, poses for a photograph in a wedding dress in 1948. (Courtesy of Art Salas.)

Libor (Saiz) García and Domitilia "Tillie" (Baca Archuleta) García on their wedding day in June 1955 in Concho. The couple married at San Rafael Catholic Church and celebrated their wedding at a nearby home. Libor is from Concho, while Tillie's family hails from Datil, New Mexico. The couple traveled with Libor's parents to Winslow to purchase Tillie's wedding dress. The couple later had 13 children. Libor is the son of Lorenzo García and Sofía García. Libor has passed away, but Tillie continues to live in Concho and is one of the oldest residents in the community. In the photograph are, from left to right, Tillie, Libor, and Margie Barreras, daughter of Greg and Sarah Barreras. (Courtesy of Angela Perea-Murphy.)

Regina Baca is seen here on the day of her wedding to Earl Wooden at Our Lady of Mount Carmel in Tempe, Arizona, on October 27, 1962. Regina sewed her own wedding dress for the occasion. She and Earl were later divorced, and she is now married to Alan Shaver. (Courtesy of Regina (Baca) Shaver.)

Filo (García) Baca and Inez (Candelaria) Baca sent their wedding photograph to her father, Pedro Román Candelaria, and her siblings Evelyn Baca, Román Candelaria, and Ralph Candelaria around 1951. The photograph was taken at Linda Studio in Winslow, Arizona. Many engaged couples traveled to Winslow for photographs and wedding attire. (Courtesy of Román Candelaria.)

Seen here are newlyweds Elsie (Barreras) Durán and Lorenzo Durán, who were married at San Rafael Catholic Church on September 13, 1959. Lorenzo was the youngest son of Abrán (Chávez) Durán and Aggie (Gonzales) Durán of Concho and Elsie was the daughter of Gregorio Barreras and Sarah (Romero) Barreras, who ran a bar and grocery store with a gas station in Concho. In the front (left to right) are flower girl Lillian Chávez, Elsie (Barreras) Durán, Lorenzo Durán, and ring bearer Robert (Durán) Smith. In the back row (left to right) are the padrinos de boda, Mary and Pitacio Martínez. Mary was Lorenzo's aunt from Winslow, Arizona. (Courtesy of Mishaela Durán.)

Arsenio (García) Ulibarrí (left) and Filomeno (García) Ulibarrí Jr. are seen here dressed up for a special occasion. Their family was from Concho, but they grew up in neighboring St. Johns. (Courtesy of Juanita (Soto) Ulibarrí.)

Filomeno (García) Ulibarrí Jr. and Juanita (Soto) Ulibarrí walk down the aisle at their wedding at Our Lady of Guadalupe Church in Holbrook, Arizona. (Courtesy of Juanita (Soto) Ulibarrí.)

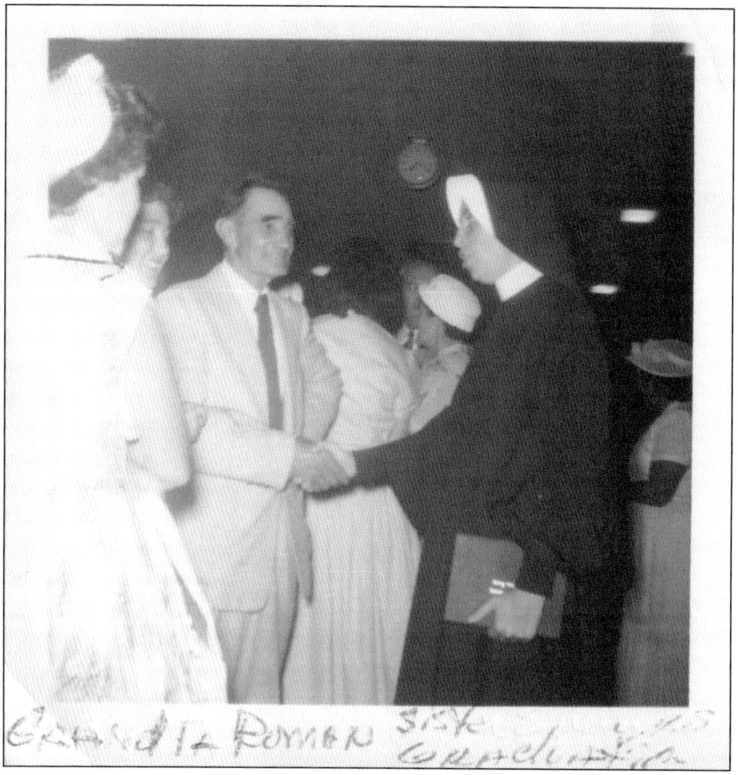

Pedro Román Candelaria (left of center) shakes hands with his daughter Evelyn Candelaria at her graduation from Loretto Academy around 1957–1958. Sister Evelyn was called from an early age to serve the Catholic Church with the Daughters of Charity, which was founded in 1633 by St. Vincent de Paul and St. Louise de Marillac. She has lived in Africa since 1974 working with the Daughters of Charity. (Courtesy of Hope MacMonagle.)

An unidentified woman is seated with Sister Evelyn Candelaria (left) looking at a book during Christmastime. (Courtesy of Regina (Baca) Shaver.)

An older woman sits next to her bed near a home altar containing images of saints, candles, and other religious items. The woman is holding a rosary. (Farm Security Administration/Office of War Information Black-and-White Negatives, Prints & Photographs Division, Library of Congress.)

Juanita Soto is seen here in a white dress and hat at a wedding service in Holbrook when she was a child. (Courtesy of Juanita (Soto) Ulibarrí.)

A Catholic saint is placed inside a wooden cabinet that is decorated with trinkets, handmade adornments, vases, a small tree with garland, and various rosaries. (Farm Security Administration/Office of War Information Black-and-White Negatives, Prints & Photographs Division, Library of Congress.)

A home altar dons the patron saint of the San Rafael Catholic Church in Concho. San Rafael is seen holding a fish used to heal Tobías in the Catholic Bible. It is common to see religious altars and imagery in the homes of many families in Concho. (Farm Security Administration/Office of War Information Black-and-White Negatives, Prints & Photographs Division, Library of Congress.)

Pictured here is the Concho School in October 1940. Children play outside. Many Concho residents fondly recall their days at this school, which served pre-high school students. Many of the school images that were captured by photographer Russell Lee in 1940 were taken here. (Farm Security Administration/Office of War Information Black-and-White Negatives, Prints & Photographs Division, Library of Congress.)

Concho School is where most of Concho's children were educated. This photograph was taken in the 1960s. The school burned down in 1984 after a kitchen fire. The gymnasium still stands, and now serves as the San Rafael Catholic Church Parish Hall. (Courtesy of Angela Perea-Murphy.)

Rosalío "Ross" F. Muñoz is at the Concho School teaching students a lesson in geography. In the photograph, he is pointing to Mexico. Although Farm Security Administration photographer Russell Lee gave generalized captions to the majority of his photographs of Concho, this photograph shows the name of student Dora Romero, who completes a math problem on the board, and Juan Padilla, whose drawing of Arizona's counties assignment hangs on the wall above the chalkboard. (Farm Security Administration/Office of War Information Black-and-White Negatives, Prints & Photographs Division, Library of Congress.)

Six students are in their classroom crouched down, playing a hunting squirrel game at Concho School in 1940. This likely is the first- through fourth-grade classroom. (Farm Security Administration/Office of War Information Black-and-White Negatives, Prints & Photographs Division, Library of Congress.)

Students are standing outside the Concho School in 1958 where generations of students were educated in two rooms—first through fourth were in one room and fifth through eighth were in another. There was no kindergarten class. Seen here is the 1958 class picture for grades first through fourth at Concho School. Pictured are, from left to right, (first row) Alex Perea, Linda Perea, Nellie Padilla, Angela Perea, Joann Sanchez, and Paul Richardson; (second row) Alex Padilla, Paula Padilla, Paula Lasher, Beverly Lasher, Judy Roebush, and teacher Audrey Waite. (Courtesy of Angela Perea-Murphy.)

Evelyn Candelaria is pictured in the first row, third from the right, at the Santa Fe St. Vincent Orphanage in 1944. The orphanage was founded in 1891 and was part of a larger facility in Santa Fe consisting of St. Vincent Hospital and the Loretto Academy. (Courtesy of Román Candelaria.)

Shown here is a young Guillermo C. Padilla in a school photograph. He is among a handful of Concho residents who have lived in the area all their lives. The Padilla family is an important part of the legacy of the community. (Courtesy of Román Candelaria.)

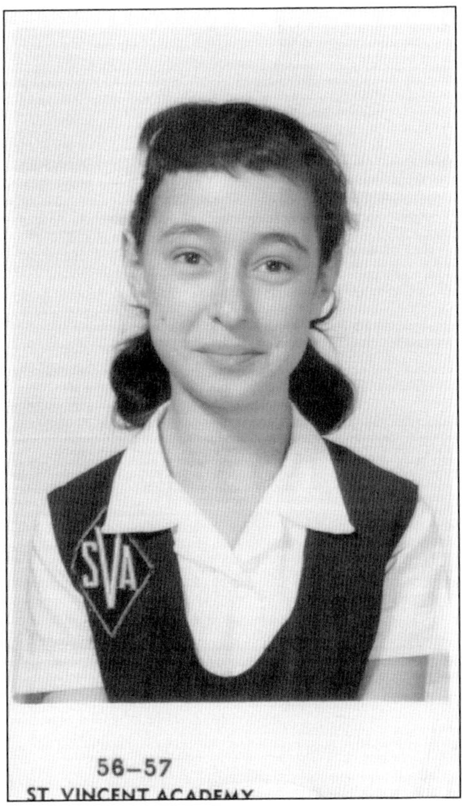

Cristóbal Maximiliano Candelaria and Marian (Baca) Candelaria's youngest daughter, Eugenia Candelaria, is pictured here at St. Vincent Academy in Santa Fe, New Mexico, during the 1956–1957 school year. (Courtesy of Román Candelaria.)

Jake Padilla (second from left), Melinda Josay, and Alex Perea are at the Concho School on stage for a graduation for the class of 1966. (Courtesy of Angela Perea-Murphy.)

Angela Perea is at her graduation from St. Johns High School. The graduating class that year included 35 students. (Courtesy of Angela Perea-Murphy.)

A young student stands at the chalkboard of the Concho School coloring in a balloon with the word "green" written inside. The students are working on simple arithmetic, spelling, and identification of words. This is likely the first- through fourth-grade classroom. (Farm Security Administration/Office of War Information Black-and-White Negatives, Prints & Photographs Division, Library of Congress.)

Four girls play on metal swings outside the Concho School in Concho in 1940. Farm Security Administration photographer Russell Lee captured in 1940 the many activities in which children participated inside and outside the classroom, showing a playful side of the community that moved beyond farm and ranch work. (Farm Security Administration/Office of War Information Black-and-White Negatives, Prints & Photographs Division, Library of Congress.)

Schoolgirls play volleyball inside the Concho School gym in 1940, which was located adjacent to the school. (Farm Security Administration/Office of War Information Black-and-White Negatives, Prints & Photographs Division, Library of Congress.)

Anita Gonzales poses for a photograph at Loretto Academy in Santa Fe, New Mexico. Many Concho residents attended private Catholic schools in New Mexico. Anita is Pedro Román Candelaria's second wife, the mother of Inez Candelaria. (Courtesy of Román Candelaria.)

Cecilia Baca is seen here at her high school graduation. She is the daughter of Gabe Baca and Ida (Candelaria) Baca. (Courtesy of Hope MacMonagle.)

Regina Baca is seen at a fashion show at Tempe Union High School around 1959. Fashion shows were quite popular across the Phoenix metropolitan area in the late 1950s, with shows organized by various women's groups. Regina was an excellent seamstress and made her own dress for the show. (Courtesy of Regina (Baca) Shaver.)

Claire Baca (left) and Carmen Baca (right) are pictured here in high school around 1959 in Tempe, Arizona. (Courtesy of Hope MacMonagle.)

Ralph Candelaria poses for a school photograph for the 1952–1953 school year. Ralph was around 16 years old in this photo. In school, he was active in sports and, during his freshman year, played football for Round Valley. (Courtesy of Román Candelaria.)

A group of young men are pictured in professional clothing. From left to right are (first row) Isidro Baca and Senito Gonzales; (second row) Pedro Román Candelaria, Ralph Candelaria, and Roger Candelaria; (third row) an unidentified Sánchez and Alejandro Carrillo. (Courtesy of Román Candelaria.)

From left to right are Liz Castillo and Kenneth Durán at the San Rafael Catholic Church Fiestas in front of the Concho School, around 1969. Liz and Kenneth were classmates and are seen here dressed in traditional costumes to perform folklórico dancing at the Fiesta. Liz's mother, Margie Castillo, was a friend of Angie (Baca) Durán, Kenneth's mother. (Courtesy of Mishaela Durán.)

High school-aged students are loading the bus that will take them to school in nearby St. Johns in 1940. The bus stop was located near the López store and service station. (Farm Security Administration/Office of War Information Black-and-White Negatives, Prints & Photographs Division, Library of Congress.)

Pictured here is the St. Johns baseball team comprised of all Hispanic players, some from Concho. From left to right (first row) Gilbert Martínez Jr., an unidentified bat boy, and Nestor Montoya; (second row) Filomeno (García) Ulibarrí Jr., Longie Vallejos, Pete Moreno, Severo Montoya, Gilbert Martínez (manager), and Manuel Ramírez; (third row) Rumaldo Baca, Ralph García, Cristóbal Ulibarrí, Jerry García, Fred Durán, Ernest Jaramillo, Boney Ramírez, Lorenzo Baca, Elías Chávez, and Marcelo Moreno. (Courtesy of Román Candelaria.)

Seen here in 1942 are (front) Seferina Raquel Baca and (back, left to right) Antonio Lorenzo Baca, Elviria (García) Baca, and Toney Baca. Toney is wearing his military uniform and was in the US Army during World War II. He enlisted along with four of his brothers, all of whom went to Europe. Antonio Lorenzo Baca owned a trucking company, and one of his trucks can be seen in the background. (Courtesy of Rudy Sánchez.)

From left to right, Alfred Padilla (front), Ralph Candelaria, and Inez Candelaria pose for a photograph in 1954. (Courtesy of Román Candelaria.)

Filomeno (Garciá) Ulibarrí Jr. is seen here in his US Marines uniform around the 1950s. Ulibarrí served in the military for three years. He is the son of Filomeno Moreno Ulibarrí and Adelaida García, whose father, Juan García, was from Concho. Filomeno and his wife, Juanita (Soto) Ulibarrí, moved to Concho from Flagstaff to live on the land his grandfather owned. (Courtesy of Juanita (Soto) Ulibarrí.)

Filomeno (García) Ulibarrí Jr. is shown in a US Marine Corps photograph in 1953, Platoon 132 in San Diego, California. Ulibarrí is on the first row, second from right, kneeling on the grass. (Courtesy of Juanita (Soto) Ulibarrí.)

Johnny López enrolled in the US Army around 1940 and went to World War II at 14 or 15 years of age. Though he was too young to enroll, he still received the GI bill and was able to pursue an education. He served as a school principal for Santa Rosa Schools in New Mexico. He married Socorro López. (Courtesy of Román Candelaria.)

Cristóbal "Criss" Polecarpio Candelaria is pictured here in his US Army uniform sometime between 1953 and 1955. (Courtesy of Román Candelaria.)

Pat Murphy is seen here in 1961, shortly after joining the US Navy. The photograph was taken when he returned from boot camp. (Courtesy of Pat Murphy).

Seen here is Hope (Baca) MacMonagle (left) with Arimando Chavarría in England around 1979–1980. MacMonagle joined the US Air Force and worked for many years as a jet engine mechanic. (Courtesy of Hope MacMonagle.)

Gabe Baca (last row, far right) is pictured here with other men from the Civilian Conservation Corps (CCC). The camp had various locations in the region, including in Springerville and McNary. The CCC had camps in the 1930s and 1940s for laborers who were not enlisted in the US Armed Forces. (Courtesy of Román Candelaria.)

Four

Leisure in Concho

As with everything, there is a season for work and for celebration. The people of Concho held several dances during the year. It was not unusual for the unwed ladies to have a chaperone. If the dances were in other towns, such as St. Johns, Holbrook, Springerville, or McNary, everyone would load up a car and go to the dance. Wedding dances were open to anyone who wanted to come and lasted until the wee hours of the morning. A renowned saxophone player from Springerville named Pulita, or Edward Sánchez, was a big attraction to any dance. Juanita and Nestor Montoya's band was also popular for special occasions.

When family and friends visited, a coffee pot was started, and cookies or other snacks were offered. Visits were used to exchange news and to share meals. When new babies came around, everyone stopped by to see the newborn and to help the mother and family in whatever way they could. The children in Concho would gather and play games like marbles, jacks, jump rope, and hide and seek. If the weather permitted, the children were allowed to go hiking and, in the fall, the boys went hunting. When a reservoir was built for Concho Creek, families would go swimming and fishing. Beginning in the early 20th century, baseball was embraced in Concho. Each town had a team and competed against each other. The games were usually held on a Sunday afternoon and everyone gathered to watch. Many Concho boys played baseball in high school in nearby St. Johns.

Socializing between families mostly occurred at church events, at homes, and in public spaces. Socializing also took place around community tasks during the harvest season. Many residents reminisce over time spent cultivating Concho chile, and families and friends would gather to string the chile into ristras. This activity, as well as others, can be seen in the photographs captured by Russell Lee (Farm Security Administration) throughout this book. Families and friends would also gather to shuck corn that would be hung or dried. Holidays, like Christmas, provided a time for lively social events, where women gathered to prepare tamales. Men would often gather at the mercantile store or bar to socialize and play cards. Even if work was the focus of the community, there was always time to enjoy the company of others.

The headwaters of the spring are seen here, around 1940, in Concho. Water was an important resource for the community, as it provided the ability to grow crops and sustain orchards, which Concho residents depended upon year after year. It also allowed them to take care of cattle, sheep, and other farm animals. Beyond its use for work, water served as a source of recreation and, in the summer months, children and young adults would play in the water and fish with their family and friends. (Farm Security Administration/Office of War Information Black-and-White Negatives, Prints & Photographs Division, Library of Congress.)

Juanita (Soto) Ulibarrí and her father, Juan Soto, sit near a river. It was common for families to spend an afternoon at the rivers or lakes nearby, with a picnic lunch and enjoying the cooler weather. (Courtesy of Juanita (Soto) Ulibarrí.)

Román Candelaria at Lyman Lake south of St. John's, Arizona, in 1958. Lyman Lake has served as a recreation spot for White Mountain communities since the early 1960s. It is the very first recreational state park in Arizona. (Courtesy of Román Candelaria.)

A young Juanita Soto is seen here with her mother Veneranda (Gurule) Soto in Holbrook, Arizona, on a bridge over the Little Colorado River in 1944. (Courtesy of Juanita (Soto) Ulibarrí.)

Siblings Raymond Soto and Juanita Soto play outside of their childhood home with their dog in Holbrook, Arizona, around 1943. (Courtesy of Juanita (Soto) Ulibarrí.)

Two unidentified young girls are seen here posing for a photograph next to chile plants in Concho in October 1940. Young children would play in the fields while their older siblings and adults tended to the crops. (Farm Security Administration/Office of War Information Black-and-White Negatives, Prints & Photographs Division, Library of Congress.)

Tomás Baca and Pedro Román Candelaria were photographed here in Springerville around 1918. The towns of Concho, St. Johns, and Springerville were well-connected, as Hispanic families who originally came from New Mexico settled in these White Mountain communities. Families and friends would visit each other often. In the same year this photograph was taken, the Spanish flu plagued Apache County and many individuals lost their lives. This photograph shows a more jovial side of that period. (Courtesy of Román Candelaria.)

From left to right, Virgie García, Emilia García, and Julia García stand together in a photograph in 1942. The girls are the daughters of Reymundo Garciá and Christina (Martínez) García. The photograph was taken in the same year that many men began leaving Concho after enlisting in the US Armed Forces during World War II. (Courtesy of Angela Perea-Murphy.)

Two of Ida (Candelaria) Baca and Gabe Baca's daughters are pictured here and provide a fun optical illusion in the photograph. Pictured are Carmen (left) and Cecilia Baca in 1956. (Courtesy of Román Candelaria.)

Seen standing are, from left to right, Gabie Baca, Cecilia Baca, Regina Baca, and Claire Baca. In the first row is their grandfather, Pedro Román Candelaria (center) with two more grandchildren seated on his lap. (Courtesy of Román Candelaria.)

Seen here are, from left to right, Telesfor Peña, Román Candelaria, and Phillip Baca on horseback. Phillip is Filo and Inez Baca's third child. The photograph was taken around 1957. (Courtesy of Román Candelaria.)

Tony Allen Baca is riding bareback on Pinto, a horse owned by Román Candelaria. Tony Allen is the son of Toney Baca. (Courtesy of Román Candelaria.)

Charlie (Gonzales) Durán (left) and Angie (Baca) Durán are pictured here around 1952. Charlie and Angie lived on the Durán family ranch in Concho after their marriage at San Rafael Catholic Church on July 19, 1952. Together, they raised eight boys, including Ruben, Louis, Kenneth, Michael, Jerry, Richard, and *cuates* (twins) Peter and Paul, all of whom received their confirmation at San Rafael. (Courtesy of Mishaela Durán.)

From left to right, Evelyn Candelaria, Pedro Román Candelaria, and Román Candelaria Jr. are pictured with their family dog Sport outside of their home on the Candelaria Ranch. (Courtesy of Román Candelaria.)

Filomeno (García) Ulibarrí Jr. (left) sits on a step in a doorway chatting with Manuel García in St. Johns, Arizona. (Courtesy of Juanita (Soto) Ulibarrí.)

Pictured are, from left to right, Paula Candelaria, Don Jesús Romero, Silvestre Candelaria, and June Candelaria. They stand outside of the Santa Anita Store in Concho on June 16, 1948. (Courtesy of Angela Perea-Murphy.)

Pictured left to right are Ralph Candelaria, Pedro Román Candelaria, Mary Ellen (McCullough) Candelaria, Santana Candelaria, Cristóbal Candelaria, and Roger Candelaria. The photograph was taken by Vidal Candelaria at the Candelaria Ranch in 1952 during a family reunion. (Courtesy of Román Candelaria.)

The Candelaria family is pictured here at the ranch. From left to right are (first row) DiMaria Candelaria and Molly Baca; (second row) Bertha Q. Candelaria, Ida (Candelaria) Baca, Pedro Román Candelaria, Cecilia Baca, and Regina Baca, who is holding her daughter Vickie Baca. (Courtesy of Regina (Baca) Shaver.)

Christina (Martínez) García (left), wife of Reymundo García (son of Tránsito and Seferina García), is seen here with her friend, Juanita Pina (right), who is sampling a cigar. (Courtesy of Rudy Sánchez.)

Pictured here are, from left to right, Regina Baca, Carmen Baca, and Claire Baca when they were working as waitress at Mugs Up Root Beer, located across from the Arizona State University stadium in Tempe, Arizona, around 1960. (Courtesy of Regina (Baca) Shaver.)

Carmen Baca (left) and Regina Baca don costumes made by Regina for an event called Carousel in Concho, Arizona, in 1959. (Courtesy of Regina (Baca) Shaver.)

Virginia "Virgie" García (left) and Flavio Ortega Jr. (right) are standing in front of poplar trees in the early 1940s outside of the residence of Frank Márquez in Concho, Arizona. (Courtesy of Rudy Sánchez.)

Four boys are photographed at a school picnic in East Fork Mission above Springerville, Arizona. From left to right are an unidentified young man, Louis "Toy" Vallejos, Emilio García, and Paul García. (Courtesy of Román Candelaria.)

Seen here from left to right are Guillermo Padilla, Román Candelaria, Cecilia Baca, and Ralph Candelaria at the Concho Creek. (Courtesy of Román Candelaria.)

Best friends Manuel Gallegos (left) and Pedro Román Candelaria sit near a field with two unidentified women. (Courtesy of Román Candelaria.)

Sonny with a cigarette! Charlie Durán was referred to as Sonny by his friends. He is seen here (second from left) with a cigarette, chatting with friends and family. The two women in the photo are likely Elsie (Barreras) Durán, who is standing with her arms crossed, and Virgie (Durán) Smith, to Elsie's right. For many families in Concho, gatherings were an opportunity to connect with loved ones, reminisce about old times, and partake in traditions that were important to them. (Courtesy of Mishaela Durán.)

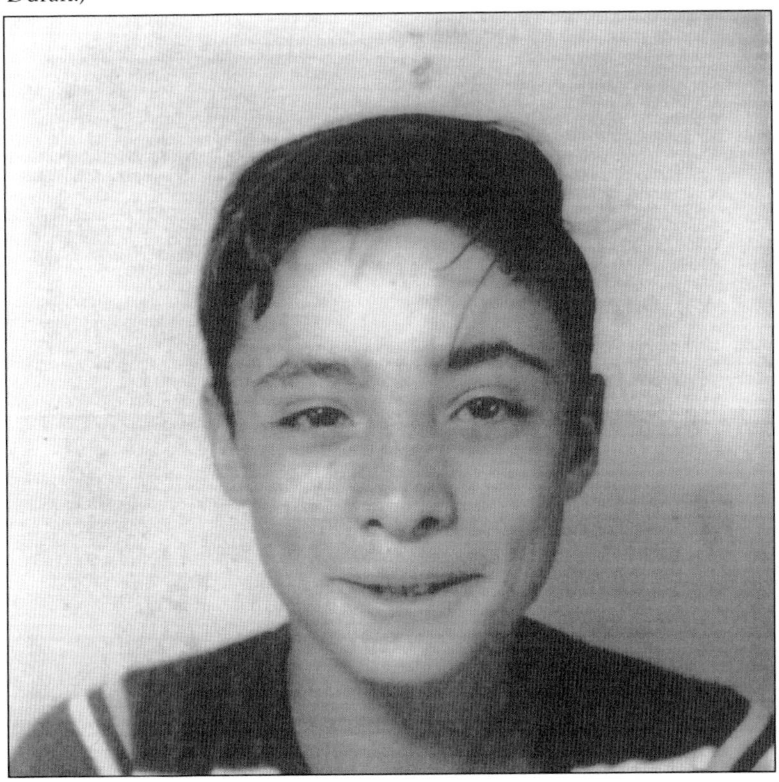

Pictured here around 1948 is Lorenzo "Lori" Durán. Lori was the son of Abrán and Aggie (Gonzales) Durán, who lived on the Durán Ranch in Concho. A story in the Durán family relates that when Abrán died, all the cattle on the ranch came out to the pasture, surrounded the ranch house, and bellowed to mourn his death. Lori was only 18 when his father passed away in 1955. (Courtesy of Mishaela Durán.)

Johnny Tapia captured this photograph of the "whole gang" in 1948. Pictured are, from left to right, (first row) two unidentified girls, Cinda (Fernández) Padilla, Pedro Román Candelaria, and Julia Candelaria; (second row) Johnny Tapia, Ralph Candelaria, Evelyn Candelaria, and Inez Candelaria. Ralph died at 18 years of age after unexpectedly going into a coma. Evelyn joined the Daughters of Charity and lived in many different places before relocating to Africa, where she still resides today. Inez married at 21 and moved away to work in the sawmills around Arizona and Oregon. (Courtesy of Román Candelaria.)

Taken around 1950, this photograph shows the widest swath of community members gathered. Pictured are, from left to right, (first row) Charlie or "Sonny" (Gonzales) Durán, Don Barreras, Lancaster "Lanky" Candelaria Jr., unidentified, Lucy Candelaria, unidentified, Emma (Durán) Padilla, and Porfie Padilla; (second row) unidentified, Pedro Román Candelaria, Preciliano Candelaria, and Johnny "Kiddy" Padilla. (Courtesy of Román Candelaria.)

Bibliography

Baca, Pauline. *Old Concho: History and Folklore*. Concho, AZ: Baca Enterprises, 2002.

Baeza, Jo. "Baca's Book a Treasure of Concho History, Folklore." *White Mountain Independent*. June 23, 2005.

Cox, Carroll. "The Last Concho Chili Farm." *White Mountain Independent*. July 2, 2003.

DeGlane, E.M., compiler. *Concho the Enchanted Pearl: A History of Concho, Arizona*. Kanab, UT: Quality Printing Co., 1981.

Obituary. Frank P. Márquez. *The Arizona Republic*, Friday, May 10, 1968: 93.

Obituary. Cecilia D. Márquez. *The Arizona Republic*, Friday, June 26, 1998: 22.

Obituary. Fr. Alfred Tachías. *The Voice of the Southwest*. Summer 2020: 7. issuu.com/voicesw/docs/summer2020/7.

Pacheco, Ana. "Santa Fe St. Vincent's Orphanage." *History in Santa Fe New Mexico*. historyinsantafe.com/nuns-in-santa-fe.

Patterson, Dolly. "Genaro Acosta–St. Johns Pioneer and Builder." *Adventures at the Museum*. apachecountyhistoricalsociety.blogspot.com.

Southern Pacific Co. v. Baca. April 5, 1954. Justia US Law. law.justia.com.

"Tempe Couple Wins $25,000 in Car-Train Crash Suit." *The Arizona Republic*. Saturday, October 23, 1954: 19.

"Train Injures Tempe Family." *The Arizona Republic*, October 19, 1951: 18.